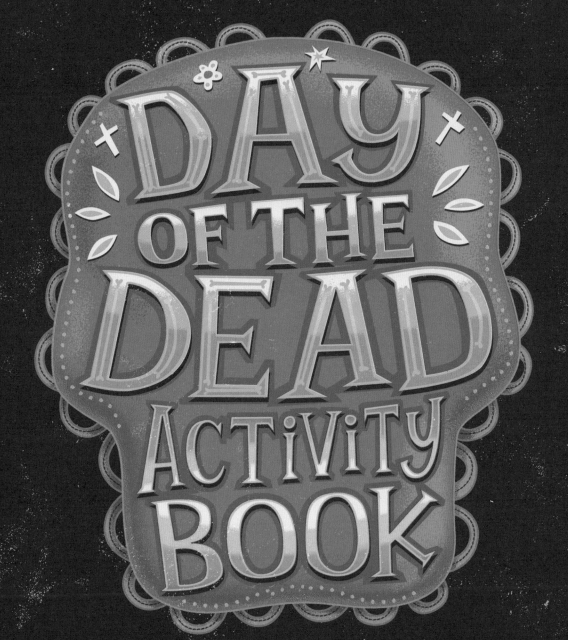

DAY OF THE DEAD ACTIVITY BOOK

by Karl Jones

illustrated by Steve Simpson

PSS!
Price Stern Sloan
An Imprint of Penguin Group (USA) Inc.

ISBN 978-0-8431-7300-0   10 9 8 7 6 5 4

ALWAYS LEARNING   PEARSON

What Is DAY OF THE DEAD?

Every year, millions of people all around the world celebrate a holiday called *Día de los Muertos*, or Day of the Dead. The celebration is all about remembering loved ones who have passed away. Each year on November 1 and 2, the departed are welcomed back to the land of the living to celebrate the best of life.

This festival has its roots in Aztec and other indigenous Latin American cultures. People honored and tended to the dead with rituals and ceremonies. Today, people celebrate by building *ofrendas* (altars) in their homes and visiting the cemeteries where their loved ones are buried. The departed are offered special food, sugar skulls, candles, and flowers. Although some symbols of the festival look spooky, it's actually a time of joy and celebration.

➡ DID YOU KNOW? ⬅

Every year, millions of monarch butterflies return to Mexico in a mass migration. It's thought that the butterflies are spirits of the dead coming back for the Day of the Dead celebrations.

What Is an OFRENDA?

An *ofrenda* is an altar or shrine built to welcome the souls returning to visit their loved ones during the Day of the Dead. *Ofrendas* are stocked with food and drinks, which the departed will need after their journey from the afterworld, and decorated with candles, flowers, photographs of the dead, and *papel picado* (decorative paper banners).

You can construct your very own *ofrenda* with the press-out pieces in this book. The activities will give you ideas about what types of offerings to make and how to decorate your *ofrenda*.

➡ DID YOU KNOW? ⬅

The celebration originally occurred during July and August, but the Spanish conquistadores changed the date to November 2 to coincide with All Saints' Day, a Catholic holy day.

Day of the Dead Maze!

This Day of the Dead family wants to visit relatives in the land of the living. Can you help them find the way?

Sugar Skulls

Have fun making and decorating sugar skulls with this easy recipe. (Make sure to ask an adult for help.) You can use the skulls to decorate your *ofrenda*.

You will need:
- ♥ 2 cups granulated sugar
- ♥ 1 egg white
- ♥ 1 tablespoon corn syrup
- ♥ ½ teaspoon vanilla extract

Makes: 3-4 two-inch skulls

Time: approx. 1 hour (and overnight)

1. Sift the sugar into a large mixing bowl.
2. In another bowl, mix the egg white, corn syrup, and vanilla extract.
3. Pour the liquid mixture into the sugar slowly. Mix by hand until a sandy dough forms.
4. Refrigerate dough for one hour. Pinch into skull shapes, or use molds to form the skulls. (Molds can be bought at specialty stores or online.)
5. Let the skulls dry overnight.
6. Once dry, decorate with icing or food coloring.

Graveyard Cake

A more recent Day of the Dead tradition includes placing chocolate coffins and skulls on the *ofrenda*. Here is a fun and easy version of a "Graveyard Cake" that you can make as part of your celebration—no baking required!

You will need:
- 2 packages (6 ounces) chocolate instant pudding mix
- 3½ cups milk (unless pudding mix calls for different amount)
- 1 package (16 ounces) chocolate sandwich cookies
- 1 tub (8 ounces) whipped cream
- 1 package tombstone-shaped cookies

Time: approx. 1 hour

1. Place the sandwich cookies in a resealable plastic bag.
   Crush them with a wooden spoon or rolling pin.
2. Prepare the pudding according to the package instructions, using the milk.
3. Let the pudding stand for five minutes.
   Add whipped cream and half of the crushed cookies.
4. Pour the mixture into a 13"x 9" pan. Spread the remaining crushed cookies over the top.
   Refrigerate for one hour.
5. Arrange the tombstone-shaped cookies to
   make the cake look like a graveyard.

Face Painting

Lots of people paint their faces for Day of the Dead celebrations. Why don't you create your own fantastic faces? You can buy face paint at arts and crafts stores or online.

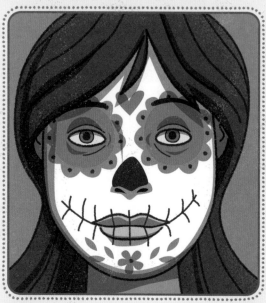

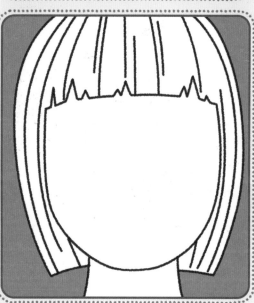

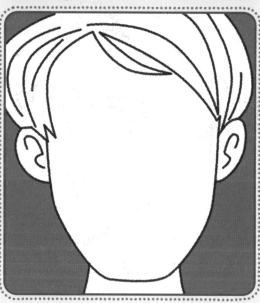

Practice your own face painting designs on the blank faces on this page.

Press-Out Face Masks

Press out the skull masks at the back of the book. Decorate them with markers, pens, or crayons. You can use the stickers included with the book to make them even more festive! Use a piece of string to tie a mask around your face, and wear it to a Day of the Dead parade or Halloween party.

Practice Your Mask DESIGN HERE!

➡ DID YOU KNOW? ⬅

Many people today wear *calaveras* (masks) to Day of the Dead celebrations and dance in honor of their deceased ancestors. The masks are often made of wood and are placed on the *ofrendas* afterward.

Word Find

Can you find these Day of the Dead words hidden below?

```
H Z D X A V O O U C R D Y E C
T T C I M D I C E Q L T M O E
W V O F T T M G I O Z O A M T
F J V I C C S O G X F O S U Z
E L D N A C X I N R E L K E A
N B X D E C R B E A U M A R P
B Y G P E A M N H O R Z W T Y
P S I I M I D K S A F C E O O
O T K K R A F Y M N U E H S A
O V U U K B S H S A L M Z R K
E P C K L Q C C A X A L G Y C
A G B V T L J V D I S B E I K
Y T U Q V S O R R M N F H K W
S K E L E T O N P A P E R N D
L D T L I K T N V F N T N Y U
```

AZTEC	MASK	MUERTOS	SKELETON
CANDLE	MEXICO	OFRENDA	SKULL
MARIGOLD	MONARCH	PAPER	SOULS

Day of the Dead Crossword

ACROSS
1. Procession of people, usually organized in a street
3. Spanish-speaking country located just south of the United States
4. Spanish word for an altar created for the Day of the Dead
5. Language spoken in most of South America
7. Day when something, such as the Day of the Dead, is celebrated
8. Month during which the Day of the Dead is celebrated
9. Relative who was born before you

DOWN
2. People encountered by Spanish explorers in what is now central Mexico
3. Flower used to decorate Day of the Dead *ofrendas*, native to North and South America
6. Popular American holiday when children dress up and go trick-or-treating

Paper Planes

These paper airplanes put a new twist on this traditional holiday! The spirits can use them to travel back and forth between the land of the dead and the land of the living.

You will need:
- ♥ black construction paper (8½" × 11")
- ♥ Crayons or chalk

1. Fold a sheet of paper in half lengthwise, and run your thumb along the fold to make a sharp crease. Unfold the paper.
2. Fold down the top corners to make two triangles at the top of the page. (They should meet on the center line.)
3. Fold the two outer edges of the paper toward the center line. Fold the plane along the center line.
4. Turn the plane sideways and create a wing crease on each side of the plane beginning at the nose of the plane.
5. Using crayons or chalk, decorate your airplane with some traditional Day of the Dead patterns and symbols. You can also use the stickers included to decorate your airplane.

Papel Picado

Use the materials below to make a colorful *papel picado* for your Day of the Dead celebration.

You will need:
colored tissue paper
(cut into 8"x 8" squares)
scissors
string
adhesive tape

1. Fold a piece of tissue paper in half from edge to edge. Repeat three or four times.
2. Cut shapes in the paper, being careful not to cut off any corners.
3. Unfold the tissue paper completely.
4. If desired, decorate the edges by cutting zigzags or fringe.

5. Fold the top of the paper (about ½ inch) over a long piece of string and tape it.
6. Use a few sheets of tissue paper to make a long streamer.

→ DID YOU KNOW? ←

Papel picado is a popular Mexican craft with Aztec roots used to make banners to decorate *ofrendas*, streets, and buildings during the Day of the Dead.

Paper Marigolds

Marigolds are an important symbol in Day of the Dead celebrations and are known as the "flower of the dead." This scent is believed to attract souls and draw them back.

You will need:
- 🤍 tissue paper
- 🤍 pipe cleaners
- 🤍 scissors

1. Fold one sheet of tissue paper in half lengthwise. Fold in half again the same way.

2. Turn the paper so that one short end is closest to you. Make a paper fan by making a fold in the end about ½ inch wide.

3. Turn your paper over and fold again, making another fold of the same size. Continue turning and folding until the entire piece of paper is folded into an accordion shape.

4.

Wrap your pipe cleaner around the middle of the tissue paper accordion. Twist it together like a twist tie, leaving a small "stem." Cut off the ends of the tissue paper on each side of your paper accordion.

5.

Fan out the accordion shape until it forms a circle. Pull up the first layer of tissue paper toward the center of the accordion and all the way around the circle. Pull up the next layer and so on. Bunch with your hands to give the flowers some texture and shape.

→ DID YOU KNOW? ←

Marigolds are native to North and South America, but are now grown all around the world.

Answer Key

WORD FIND, PAGE 10:

```
H Z D X A V O O U C R D Y E C
T T C W M D I C E Q L T M O E
W V O F T T M G I O Z O A M T
F J V I C C S O G X F O S U Z
E L D N A C X I N R E L K E A
N B X D E C R B E A U M A R P
B Y G P E A M N H O R Z W T Y
P S I I M I D K S A F C E O O
O T K K R A F Y M N U E H S A
O V U U K B S H S A L M Z R K
E P C K L Q C C A X A L G Y C
A G B V T L J V D I S B E I K
Y T U Q V S O R R M N F H K W
S K E L E T O N P A P E R N D
L D T L W K T N V F N T N Y U
```

CROSSWORD, PAGE 11:
ANSWERS: 1A: parade, 2D: Aztecs,
3A: Mexico, 3D: marigold, 4A: *ofrenda*,
5A: Spanish, 6D: Halloween, 7A: holiday,
8A: November, 9A: ancestor

Build Your Own Ofrenda!

Now it's time to build your own Day of the Dead shrine.

Step 1
Press out piece 1 (the front). With the candles, marigolds, and skulls facing out, fold along the scored lines. Press out piece 2 (the base), and with the stone pattern facing up, fold up along the scored lines. Insert the three front tabs of piece 2 into the bottom slots of piece 1.

Step 2
Press out piece 3 (the left wall with the large flower). With the green side facing out, fold along the scored lines. Attach piece 3 to pieces 1 and 2 by inserting the tabs into the slots.

Step 3
Press out piece 4 (the right wall with the skull and floral head arrangement). With the green side facing out, fold along the scored lines. Then attach piece 4 to pieces 1 and 2 by inserting the tabs into the slots the same way you did in the previous step.

Step 4
Press out piece 5 (the top shelf and partial back). With the stone top facing out, fold along the scored lines. Attach piece 5 to pieces 1, 3, and 4.

Step 5
Insert the two remaining tabs of pieces 3 and 4 into the slots in piece 5.

Step 6
Press out piece 6 (the cross) and insert the bottom tab into the slot at the top of piece 1.

Piece 1 (the front)

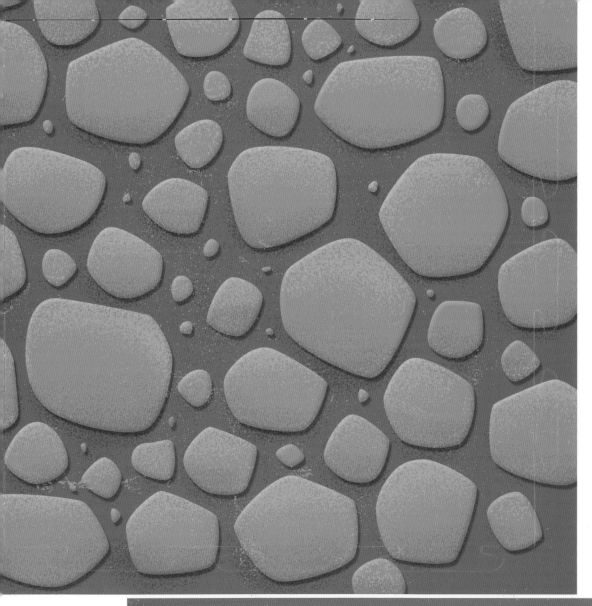

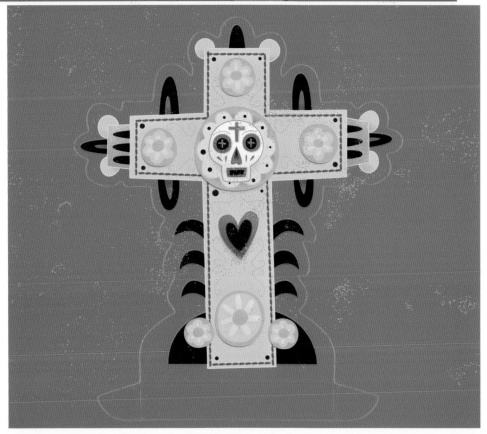

Piece 3 (the left wall)

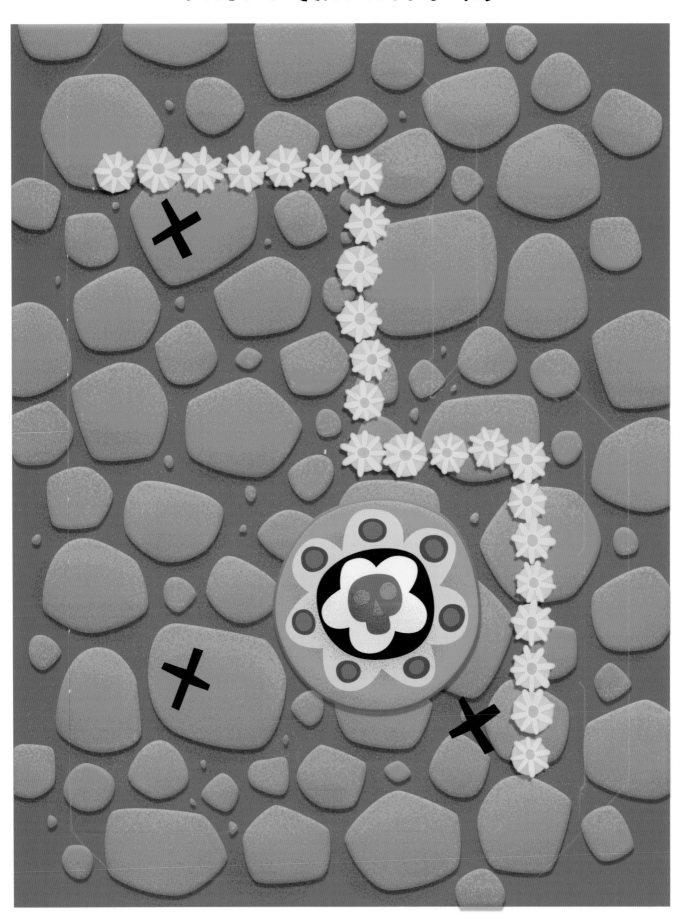

Piece 4 (the right wall)

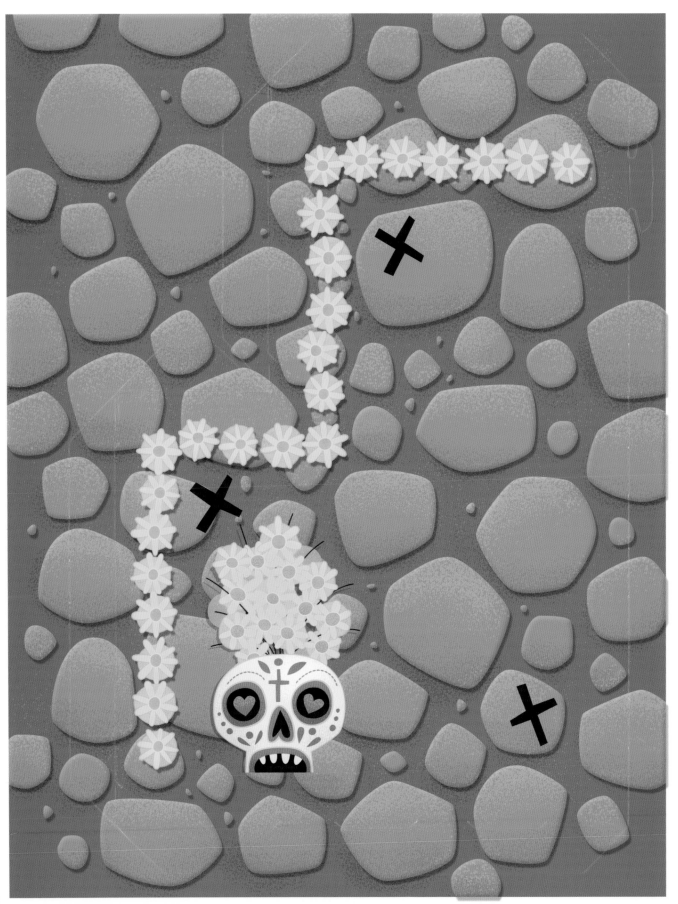

Piece 5 (the top)

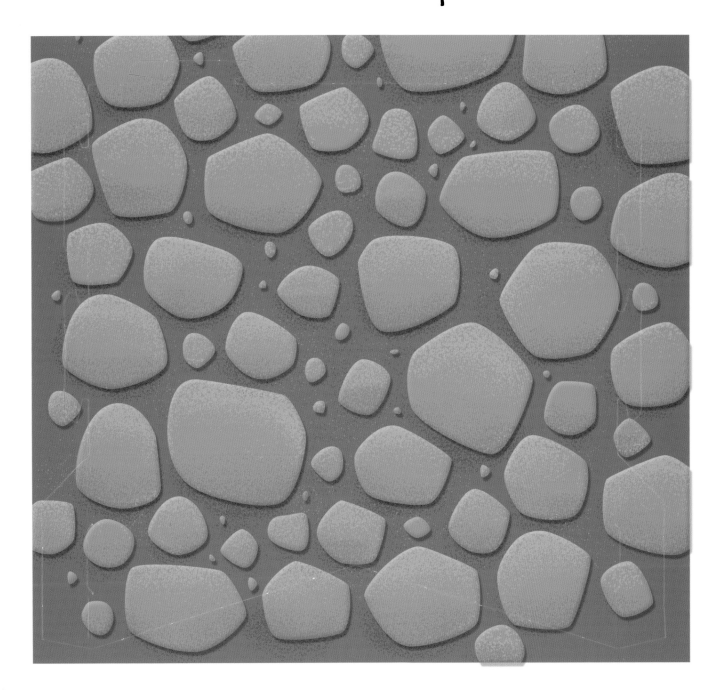

Make Your Own Mask

Decorate your Day of the Dead mask. Press out the mask along the perforated lines.
Attach string to both sides of the mask to tie around your head and wear on the Day of the Dead!

Make Your Own Mask

Decorate your Day of the Dead mask. Press out the mask along the perforated lines.
Attach string to both sides of the mask to tie around your head and wear on the Day of the Dead!

Press out these
figures and stands
and slot them together
so your figures stand up.

© by Steve Simpson